VOX

John R. Szymanski, BS
Your Last Poet

An Autobiographical Warning

John R. Szymanski, BS

PAGE PUBLISHING
Conneaut Lake, PA

First originally published by Page Publishing 2024

ISBN 979-8-89157-893-7 (pbk)
ISBN 979-8-89157-919-4 (digital)

Printed in the United States of America

Yeshu Mihal
Omaha, Nebraska
1981

Everything is the opposite of what it seems.
The Almighty works through human agents.
The Jesus dynasty is a family affair.
VOX is the Latin form for "voice."
Can there be a "rational suicide?"
Just be just.

CONTENTS

BIOGRAPHY

I am a bachelor, born in Detroit, Michigan. During high school, I excelled in varsity football. As a magna cum laude graduate from college, I earned my living working in the Detroit automotive marketing field. I also earned my real estate appraiser's license and enjoy teaching the guitar. I have traveled extensively throughout the States and Mexico. Both East and West Coasts have been my destinations, from Daytona to Venice beaches.

I am passionate concerning esoteric studies. I've attended churches, mosques, and synagogues while embracing shamanism, Buddhism, and Taoism. I am a burly man. My brush cut hair is coarse, and my skin adapts easily to the Pacific Northwest climate. I enjoyed reading the written words of the desert mystics, Anthony the Great, Macarius the elder, and Evagrius Ponticus.

My future plans involve adding a new perspective to literature by providing a fresh vantage point into a purer, cleaner realm of writing. Someday, I look forward to the majesty of the desert, where the air is purer, the sky more limpid, and God is closer. The opportunity to leave the tumult of the city, to seek a "creative quietude" would indeed be a sought-after accomplishment.

John R. Szymanski, BS
Warren High Varsity Football Team
1975

ANSWERS

I am eager to work in the desert. The opportunity to leave the tumult of the city, to seek creative solitude, would indeed be a sought-after accomplishment.

The Ellen Meloy fund will be helpful to pay for round-trip transportation and camping expenses for conducting my research at Death Valley National Park.

My desert experiences include camping in the desert during a trip from Los Angeles to Las Vegas. I also enjoyed camping, during a visit to Carefree, Arizona. This endeavor included fasting, camping, and hiking.

My Death Valley National Park experience will be a precursor for Ein Gedi, Dead Sea, Israel. This accomplishment will lead to what Carlos Casteneda calls a "man of knowledge."

EXPLANATIONS

VOX will add new perspectives to desert literature by providing a fresh vantage point into a purer, cleaner realm of writing. This would include sensory deprivation, silent meditation, and fasting. Desert literacy will be advanced by providing a new ascetic point of view for the twenty-first century.

Alumni Profile

Your Guitar Man

Alum travels the country and finds true passion. By Ashley Lee Mittelmeier

John Szymanski '80 is Adrian College's guitar man. Quite literally, as his business is called "Your Guitar Man."

John is an instructor who goes to the homes of his students, who range in age from seven to 62 years old, to share his passion of the guitar and teachs them how to play.

Even though he began studying the guitar at age 12, he didn't really begin to focus on it until after he graduated from Adrian. It took him awhile to get where he is today.

"As an undergraduate, I envisioned my career as a dentist," he said. "Yet, what I was really doing was living in the shadow of someone else's dream."

John was academically competing with his high school valedictorian who went on to Harvard Medical School. As a senior at AC, John lost all interest in sciences and shifted direction to business.

"As you can see, I was on the medical track and did very well in my science courses," John says as he proudly displays a copy of his College transcript that showed nothing lower than a B in any class.

John is a spiritual man and is intrigued by great philosophers. He took comfort in this way of thinking as a student.

"In Ann Arbor, I identified with the academics/poets of Arthur Rimbaud," he said. "This led to Nietzsche, Kierkegaard and Sartre. I found great comfort in Lao Tse, shamanism and the Gnostic Mandaeans."

John ended up graduating magna cum laude with a Bachelor of Science degree in biology and business.

John's long journey to "Your Guitar Man" started here. On April 27, 1980, he stood proudly in his black cap and gown holding his diploma.

Four years, later when he was supposed to be in grad school, he found himself playing the guitar and selling suntan oil from the trunk of his car in Daytona Beach, Florida.

"I went from beta beta business to beta beach and babes," he jokes.

John has a great sense of humor, but after meeting him, discovered he has a great sense for adventure and the unknown. He was just living the dream.

"From Daytona Beach I headed west making many stops along the way, eventually settling in Redondo Beach, California, working for the FDA," he said.

After traveling across the country, he returned home to Pontiac where he worked in automotive marketing and consumer relations for Ford, Volkswagen and EDS for a decade.

Fast-forward another three years and this is when John began his career as a guitar instructor.

"Teaching is all I do now," he says. "Music is important to me because it's easy, fun and very rewarding."

John's musical background is classic rock. He loves Led Zeppelin, Alice Cooper and the Rolling Stones. Throughout his travels he had the honor of meeting each of the Rolling Stones.

"It's a bit challenging because kids today like the music of Lincoln Park and Green Day and I'm not familiar with them," he said. "But I do the best I can to teach the students what they're interested in. I use YouTube to research the songs, buy the sheet music and go from there."

As John begins a new chapter in his life, now living in Royal Oak where he travels to teach 20 students full time, he often thinks of his time at Adrian College.

"AC was a smart decision for me," he said. "I still remain close with lifelong friends **Brian VanRiper '80** and **Greg Westcott '81**."

Although the path was long, John couldn't be happier than where he is today.

"I've realized I'm not a 'nine to five' guy," he says. "Teaching is much more fun and I can see myself doing this for a long time."

"I went from beta beta business to beta beach and babes."

John is holding a bookpicker guitar which is designed to be played around campfires. He says it's the easiest to use for teaching and taking to his students' homes.

ADRIAN COLLEGE

Adrian, Michigan

Name	SZYMANSKI, JOHN RICHARD
Address	26VA Laurel …
	Warren, Michigan 48092
Birth Date	6/24/58 Place Detroit, Michigan
Parent or Guardian	Mr. & Mrs. Richard L. Szymanski
Date of Admission	September 1976
From	Warren Sr.H.S., Warren, Michigan
Conditions	

Degrees and Certificates

Bachelor of Science - April 27, 1980 magna cum laude

Major Biology

Teaching Minor Business

Faculty Action

GRADING SYSTEM   A = 4.0   C = 2.0   F = 0.0 (falling)
B = 3.0   D = 1.0   I = 00 (Incomplete)

P = Satisfactory progress achieved. Does not affect grade point average.
NC = Indicates no credit and applies to English 101 only.
WP = Authorized withdrawal after end of change of course period. Achievement passing
WF = Authorized withdrawal after end of change of course period. Achievement failing
Granted Honorable Dismissal Unless Otherwise Stated By Faculty Action

Date: 5-17-89   Registrar:

Dept	Course Number	Course Title	Sem. Hours	Grade	Grade Points	Grade Average	Dept	Course Number	Course Title	Sem. Hours	Grade	Grade Points	Grade Average
76330		SZYMANSKI JOHN R			F	76	76330		SZYMANSKI JOHN R			F	77
BIOL	111H	EXPER DESIGN	1	A+	4		ECON	202	PRIN MACROECON	3	A+	12	
PSYC	100	GEN PSYCHOLOGY	3	A+	12		B AD	100	PRIN OF BUSINESS	3	A	12	
BIOL	101H	PRIN OF BIOLOGY	3	A	12		CHEM	103	COLL CHEMISTRY	4	A	16	
MATH	101	INT COLL ALGEBRA	4	A	16		PHYS	101	INTRO PHYSICS	4	B+	12	
ENGL	101	TOPICS IN WRIT	3	A-	12								
ADRIAN COLLEGE		SEMESTER TOTALS	14	14	56	4.00	ADRIAN COLLEGE		SEMESTER TOTALS	14	14	52	3.71
ADRIAN, MICH.		CUMULATIVE TOTALS	14	14	56	4.00	ADRIAN, MICH.		CUMULATIVE TOTALS	45	45	176	3.91
76330		SZYMANSKI JOHN			I	77	76330		SZYMANSKI JOHN R			S	78
INTM	123	ACAROLOGY	2	A	8		ECON	201	PRIN MICROECON	3	A	12	
							PHYS	102	INTRO PHYSICS	4	A	16	
							CHEM	104	COLL CHEMISTRY	4	A	16	
							BIOL	360	COMP VERT ANAT	4	B	12	
ADRIAN COLLEGE		SEMESTER TOTALS	2	2	8	4.00	ADRIAN COLLEGE		SEMESTER TOTALS	15	15	56	3.73
ADRIAN, MICH.		CUMULATIVE TOTALS	16	16	64	4.00	ADRIAN, MICH.		CUMULATIVE TOTALS	60	60	232	3.86
76330		SZYMANSKI JOHN R			S	77	76330		SZYMANSKI JOHN R			F	78
BIOL	226	PLANT BIOLOGY	4	A	16		CHEM	313	ORGAN CHEM LAB	1.0	A-	4	
MATH	105	PRE-CALC MATH	5	A	20		ACCT	203	PRIN ACCT I	3.0	A	12	
ENGL	110	TOPICS IN LIT	3	A-	12		CHEM	311	ORGANIC CHEM	3.0	A	12	
PSYC	203	ABNORMAL PSYCH	3	A-	12		BIOL	365	VERTEBRATE PHYS	3.0	A	12	
							BIOL	211	HUMAN GENETICS	3.0	A+	12	
							BIOL	367	VERTE PHYS LAB	1.0	A	4	
ADRIAN COLLEGE		SEMESTER TOTALS											

THE ROAD TO JERUSALEM

Sex was invented by the first shaman. You may ask yourself, What is a shaman? A shaman is the arch typical technician of the sacred, and his realm is specifically the relationship between the mythic imagination and ordinary consciousness. A shaman knows himself by divine appointment (i.e., hearing the call of the road). This original long-hair, wearing leather clothes, would dance possessed to the rhythms being banged out on a drum. The shaman is a much too dangerous character to have in the neighborhood. He is often alone, a half-mad loner through whom a god, or a demon, may begin speaking unexpectedly, not at all keeping with orderly social processes.

The shaman, who has been elected by the spirits, shows obvious symptoms. He becomes extremely nervous and withdrawn ("willed introversion" is the first sign of genius) and begins to act strangely and unpredictably. Shamans are sensitive individuals who suffer from an extremely labile nervous system. This condition would not be considered degenerative or pathological, rather an invitation to shamanize, to grow with the condition constitutes the cure.

Shamans clearly have access to dimensions of consciousness unavailable to the general public. In our culture, this condition is regarded as a psychotic exasperation. Yet the shaman is not psychotic; he is completely functional and most often the most intelligent and creative soul in the neighborhood. Since he has suffered psychic maiming and was able to overcome it, he can now cure others afflicted by similar conditions.[1] Jesus demonstrated the shamanic characteristics of a vision quest by fasting in the desert, then healing people who had faith in Him.

Shamans like the sun. "Helios Apotheosis" is divinization into the suntan king. Although much shamanic work is done at night, or with eyes closed, absorbing sunlight is an important part of his life. Typically, shamans enjoy being in the sun for hours, collecting and storing energy for their nocturnal activities. Many ancient shamans were sun worshippers, who appeared to stare directly into the sun, to receive it's benefits.[2] The most perfect state of being is "having sunshine for lunch," known as breatharianism, or "living on solar radiation."[3]

William James, in his book entitled, *The Varieties of Religious Experience*, states that an individual with a "quirky disposition with the ability to associate by similarity, has the correct constitution to make a mark on the age."[4] You may ask yourself, What is an age? Our sun revolves in reverse order of the zodiac, comprised of twelve ages, approximately 2,100 years each. The sun moved into the age of Taurus in approximately 4200 BC, when historic Adam was on the planet. During the life of Abraham, 2100 BC, the sun moved into the age of Aries. Jesus walked the planet at the beginning of the Piscean age. Earth is now standing at the cusp of the Piscean-Aquarian age. Aquarius is the eleventh sign of the zodiac, associated with bad omens, sinners, destruction, and penance. It's symbol is the "water bearer."[5] The shamanic personality correlates to James's description of the "quirky disposition."

Jim Morrison stated that he wanted to hear the last words of the last poet. The last poet will be breatharian, where black is the color and none is the number. Morrison was the enigmatic lead singer for the rock-in-roll outfit called the Doors. My initiation to existentialist thought began by reading his biography entitled *No One Here Gets Out Alive.* Morrison described himself as the "key to the labyrinth."[6] He was precisely as he mentioned, because it was my investigation of Morrison that led me down "the road to Jerusalem." James Douglas Morrison died at the age of twenty-seven from heart failure, in Paris, 1971.

Morrison was influenced by the nineteenth-century French symbolist poets, Charles Baudelaire and Arthur Rimbaud. Baudelaire and Rimbaud lived lives of debauchery. Baudelaire stated, "I have felt the wind of madness pass over me!" Rimbaud was born on October 20, 1854, in Charleville, France. He was an honor student in school.

He crafted his poetry between the ages of sixteen and nineteen and never composed afterward. Rimbaud traveled all over Europe and Africa. He worked as coffee and gun trader before dying on November 10, 1891, in Marseilles from a worsened condition of a leg tumor. Rimbaud stated, "My eternal soul, redeem your promise, in spite of the night alone, and the day on fire."[7]

Morrison was also influenced by the existentialist themes of Jean-Paul Sartre, who claimed, "My existence is absurd!" Sartre's existentialism begins with the forerunning thoughts of Soren Kierkegaard and Friedrich Nietzsche. Kierkegaard contributed his philosophical ideas of the "leap of faith," and the three stages of Christian life: aesthetic, ethical, and religious. There can be a teleological suspension of the ethical stage. Kierkegaard states that the ultimate Christian experience is martyrdom.[8]

Nietzsche is best known for his ideas about the "will to power," the "*ubermensch*," and the "death of God." The idea about the death of God is perhaps one of his most compelling philosophical contributions. In his book entitled *The Joyful Wisdom*, Nietzsche presents the story of the madman who announces to the morning crowd that "God is dead!" By the death of God, Nietzsche means the death of society's belief in God. However, this will enable society to lose its childlike dependency upon God. Human beings must now find the courage themselves to be gods in a world without God. Now the greatest need is to develop a new type of individual, the ubermensch, who will be strong and morally and intellectually independent. The only morality of the ubermensch will be to affirm life, to be powerful, free, joyous, and creative.

The ubermensch can survive only by human selection, eugenic foresight, and a strict education. Yet a school where one can laugh heartily, asceticism of the will, but no condemnation of the flesh. The dominant mark of this type of man will be the love of danger and strife, provided that they have a purpose.

I appreciate Nietzsche's thoughts about the "death of God." I trust that God is nowhere (as in "now here"). However, one must acknowledge that this mystery called God literally spoke in the creation of the planet Earth (Genesis 1:3). The "will to power" is another one of Nietzsche's many contributions to philosophy. The *world* and *flesh* became synonyms of *evil*, and poverty as a proof of virtue. This gave rise to the master-slave morality. Behind all this supposed morality is a secret "will to power."

I acknowledge, accept, and trust in God's new creation: risen Christ. Jesus is recognized as Logos, second person of the Trinity, second Adam/Moses, Son of God/Man, and Christ (Messiah). In short, Jesus manifests divino-human reality. Jesus is aware of His identification and mission as Savior. Jesus identifies the temple with His father's house (Luke 2:49). Jesus demonstrates no reaction at His baptism (Luke 3:21–22). Jesus identifies Himself as the "Son of Man" and assumes the authority to forgive sins (Luke 5:24). Jesus's self-awareness is healthy, illustrated by His prodigious activities and veracious doctrine. Consider that Jesus was reluctant at the beginning and end of His career. "My hour has not yet come" and "Father, if You will, remove this cup from Me." By completing His first miracle, changing water into wine at the Cana wedding, Jesus realized that He was essentially embarking on a "rational suicide" mission. He actually orchestrated His own execution! Yet by obeying the Father's will through crucifixion, the Messiah fulfilled His earthly mission.

SEASON FOR A SAVAGE: SOUL ALCHEMY

"Season for a Savage: Soul Alchemy" are the reflections of a hedonistic libertine (silent watchman). It is a story of desperation yet intended to be a "song of hope."

SEED

Seed passing through
Water well
Ravaged shell
Rising angel

"Seed" is my interpretation of the parable of the sower and the seed. Man may be viewed as a seed sown (thrown) into this world. The human condition is analogous to seed germination. The shell represents the human body. Frustration with myself and mainstream moderationalists, due to family and school expectations, occurred, in the early 1980s, while attending the University of Michigan School of Dentistry. To escape this dilemma, I became enamored with the artistry of Jim Morrison and the Doors. I ardently scrutinized the French existentialism of Jean-Paul Sartre and the symbolist poetry of Arthur Rimbaud. Shortly thereafter, I quietly left Ann Arbor, Michigan. Still perceiving myself as a scientist, I then embarked upon an exploration, utilizing myself and America as my laboratory.

LA GHETTO: WILDERNESS

Wander in the wilderness
Metamorphose to majestic desperado
Contemplate moral integrity

"Wilderness" is a bid to take a walk on the wild side, an invitation to endure the poverty of street life, then contemplate exactly what activities one would or wouldn't pursue for survival. Reflections on downtown Los Angeles and the strangers I associated with. Washing dishes in a ghetto retirement home for shelter. My fellow employees were drifters, like myself, yet they all believed that they were undiscovered stars just on the brink of fame and fortune.

DAYTONA FUGITIVE: NIGHT

Tonight prowled along pier
Craved tongue inside ear
Headlight sounds, Darwin near?
Close eyes, day disappears

Dig the pounding drum
Nightmare has now begun
Plunge wide, deep inside
Jeans wet beneath tide

Purity of vision, near and far
Slept too long beneath these stars
Getting cold now. Jesus?
Look within to find Him

Now night envelops the town

"Daytona Fugitive: Night" is the struggle to see beyond the ephemeral. Recollections of a typical Daytona Beach night. The evening begins prowling the beach for action and concludes asleep in a parking lot. "Freefalling sensations" (dream), carefree itinerancy, the thrill of a "fugitive stage performance" (male variety), serenity of the public library, my heart bleeding through my 55' telecaster upon the beach house rooftop, savoring a maduro (nightmare) intrastate hitchhiking, "death stalks the highway," paying the price to "lost angels."

BREATH OF FRESH AIR

Backstreets, alleyways, strippers, whores
Stage kicks; library solitude
The rooftop
Purple jack visions; cigars and guitars
The beach

"Lost Angels" extending assistance and refuge. Pay the price for their "generosities."

TAMPA OUTLAW: RADIANT MIND

Warren winds blow
Sunshine on your face
Rising rainbow
Perfect health & chaste

Broken heart manifests in a frenzy. Lost weekend, night prowl. "Break on through to the other side?" Welcome to crisis ward number 9, Horizon Hospital. Policeman's handcuffs removed, cringed, noting fellow inmates climb walls while shambling the "Haldol shuffle." For you have heard, "I have felt the wind of madness pass over me!"

MICHIGAN REHABILITATION: ROGUE

Concept of outlaw: barbarian, desperado
In short, a rogue
Who are these outsiders, and where do you find them?
Rogue is always the most feared one amongst the townspeople

Burn in wind, fly through night
Endless journey to gain insight

Travel through labyrinths of time and space
Traverse depths of paranoia, taste crippling crypts of
Negative assumption
Touch unification state, fusion into absolute oneness of
Ecstasy

Who is this American enigma?
Lurking outside, searching within
Who heard him?

Glimpse the glimmer of the perimeter. For you have heard, "In the perimeter there are no stars, out there one is all alone." Clinton Valley, Madison Hospitals; neuroleptic injections seal wounded mind. Jammin' with fellow inmates. Penny and my parents' deaths, cloistered nuns, power in prayer, repent sins, not dreams.

PONTIAC REHABILITATION: ROGUE

Idea of outlaw: barbarian, dancer, scientist
In short, a rogue
Who are these outsiders, and where do you find them?
Rogue is always the most feared one, amongst neighbors

Burn in wind, fly through night
Endless journey to gain insight

Travel through labyrinths of time and space
Traverse "mind lock's terror"
Taste crippling crypts of negative assumption
Touch realization state
Fusion into absolute oneness of ecstasy

Who is this American enigma?
Lurking outside, searching within
Who heard him?

"Rogue" is my ego identification and endurance of emotional extremities.

NEW DAWN

Two eyes rise from the east
Verily stranger the angel is a beast
Shall we fast before the feast?

Ravaged heart, destitute in darkness
Wounded soul, welcome home today
I've wandered in the wilderness
Now I learn to pray

"No eternal reward forgives us for wasting the dawn"
Awake with the sun…A new dawn is upon us

When venturing to "ride the snake," one either grasps at insights, or as in my case, may be regarded as a "pure idiotae" (towering fool). There is no place for a "shithouse poet" in this world; it belongs to the engineer. My "season to burn" is over. I now commence my "season to learn." Bury the dead. One must be absolutely modern.

I consider myself a freethinker. Preferring a pragmatic/gnostic approach to the Catholic mind. In short, the task at hand is not the talk, but rather the walk. I deem that things are not what they seem. One cannot hope to arrive without exile. To attain truth, one must be able to demarcate false. Conceive a ghetto mansion vs. luxury prisons. Discipline manifests freedom. Let us not own wooden barns in the sand, but rather, create a kingdom on the rock.

SEASON FOR A SAVAGE: LYCANTHROPY

Strive to be a functional individual, in control of environment. For you have heard, "My eternal soul, redeem your promise, in spite of the night alone, and the day on fire!" and "The world is just a little town" and "Past, present, and future are illusions, if stubborn ones." Now I tell you this: One can't hope for health without enduring a "season for a savage." Lycanthropy: "Who can wage war against a beast except a beast?" The art of war is imperative to state. If you think that the serpent will bite you, *those snakes will bite you*! The human condition is analogous to seed germination.

UNDER THE BOOTS OF
THE SILENT WATCHMAN

Please allow me to introduce myself…dark chant o' despair, song o'
hope.

SEED

Seed passin' through
H2O well
Ravaged shell
Burnin' hell

IDLE MIND

Pill no swallo'
Tremblin' waters, no taste
Blinded by rainbo'
Devastation 'n' waste

NIGHT

Tonight wandered along pier
Craved tongue inside ear
Headlight sounds Darwin near
Close eyes, day disappear

Dig poundin' drum
Nightmares begun
Plunge wide-deep inside
Jeans wet beneath tide

Vivid lucidity, near 'n' far
Slept II long beneath stars
Gettin' cold
Look within II find him:
Night envelops town

IDEA

What's d idea
Eternal idea
Heroes' idea-pride-intellect-energy
Actuality consists o' mobile idea
Idea conflicts create war
Art o' wars imperative to state
Idea stands, falls on fruits
Appearances derived idea
Universe appears not w/o seer
Glimpse Almighty's imperial rain
Glimpse glimmerin' perimeter beyond man's on own
Man's fall coincides w/ farmin'
Own not castles in the sand, create room IV thought
Consider luxury prisons-lake privileges
Consider somatic extremity-o'-empirical paradox
Consider hedonistic libertine
No arrival w/o exile
Rogue's idea-detach-yes-profit
Wish u well

ROGUE

Outlaw's idea-barbarian-bigman-dancer
In short, rogue
Whore dees loaners-lost-'n'-found
Rogues most feared amongst villagers

Burn in the wind, fly through the night
Watchdog paths insight
Traverse labyrinths space-time
Mindlock's terror, cripplin' crypts
Ecstasy's oneness—vivid lucidity

Who's d enigma
Lurkin' outside, lookin' within
Who heard him?

THIEF IN THE NIGHT

"There must be someway outta here," said joker to thief
Last poet is a thief of fire
"Get not excited," thief kindly joked
Prometheus stole fire from heaven
Yeshu was crucified amongst thieves
There's a thief in the temple…at midnight

ODE TO A BURNING BRIDGE

Without crosses to carry and beasts of burden to bear
We dance on this stage called life
From folly to Nazarite hair

When acquiring worldly gold, dem lose the desire
For building mysteries untold
Babylon's bridge is on fire

So I journey on alone, Lord
Trust ravaged heart shall reap life's richest reward

While fisherking irons sol like a "shattered arrow"

I tell you: "Break on through, children of tomorrow

The Zion train is coming our way
And I'm a-gonna be iron, like a lion in Zion

OUR 2 LITTLE SABRAS

Earth gig is temporal…nuclear
Warzone of shadows…full-o'-fear
Still, listening to her…reading me
Makes me do my best…kid

Witness a bedroom at dawn's breaking light
Beast dog in black…his angel butterfly in white
And our 2 little sabras, just happy, forever with us

Such mythic unions do exist
Let's not run from ourselves
Like kisses to moonlight grenades
Terrifying leap to journey within yourself
A phantom's labyrinthian maze

Just the voice of Johanna, without her
Darling, what's this heart a-gonna do
Still, mystically dear (in my mind's eye)
Dog 'n' butterfly are one

I know I can't always get what I want
Yet most times I get just what I need
And those 2 little sabras (for now)
Remain a glimmer' lost in my eyes

ABAKULU MUNDI: HELIOS APOTHEOSIS

Dawn-enter deathtown
Folly
Loneliness
Willed introversion
Asceticism
Great noon-enter sandman
Shadows hour-gig
Sundown hour-gig
Night-awkward instant
Mourning hour-streets
New breath-enter birthtown

VOICE OF ARMAGEDDON

Deutschland will lead the European aggression towards
Jerusalem, from the West
China will attack Jerusalem from the east
Russia will invade Jerusalem from the north
Egypt will lead the Islamic invasion of Jerusalem from the
South

The inherent evil that brought hell to this Earth will surface
once again

ALL ALONG ISAIAH 21

(Looking East From Calhoun Square)

Wander in the wilderness
Plato's static world is by far the best
Until its other side reveals Deb's little black dress
And a loose obedience to Kali's white vegetable king law

Wander in the wilderness
Metamorphose to majestic desperado
Beyond the valley of Aenon
Where one becomes two

DAYBREAK

Sol rises from east
Verily angel's a beast
Fast-feast

Ravaged heart—destitute-i'-darkness
Wound sol-welcome home today
Wander-i'-wilderness
Learn-'n'-prey

Forbid not, wastin' dawn
Awake with sun
New dawn ours

Return to caves
Control environment confront void
Tomorrow, enter birthtown
Paths' preparation imperative to state

Who will run with hunt?

In gig like dis, partnerships impossible
Dem among us feel life's a joke
Dem dat dig, dig it

II
IV

MARY

When I think of Mary
Warren winds cry through and through
Because in my heart…there's always you

There's a sincerity about her
As Warren shall win
Because we are confident in the victory
Of bad over evil

I'm a lion and I'm a lamb
And I'm diggin' in
There's just one secure spot on this planet
There's no room at the inn

After my roadwork, I walk again
I'm a-homecoming to the "queen o' hearts"
And I belong in the service o' the queen
Me 'n' Mary made a beautiful team
While she's been nursing

I've been thinking
I am fatal wound healing

ELYSIAN FIELDS FOREVER

It's all about fatal wound healing
Who wears the queen's ring?
He wanders a dead shoreline
Season for a noble savage
His skin leathered from sunshine
Last poet on the rampage

He's been crippled from fear
It killed his love for her
Now he feels no fear
I'm just waiting on a friend…in disguise
Verily, wealth is not measured in gold
Only words from Sol
Now slide on this:

Plato's world is static
Welcome to nightmare number 9
Welcome to a spiv's fifth damnation
Welcome to this bard's Elysian Field

Warning

When attempting to glimpse alleged Elysian Field, overstand that "out there" (on the other side), there are no stars/connections. "Out there" (here), beyond the perimeter, a white slave-driving downpressor eternally strikes black water goats! Since these hounds "dig it" when the whip comes down, the spirit of gravity simply makes a crying clown of himself Now as these "regal beagles" bark across the arc of heaven, the sign of fisherking arises, as night rains across an eastern sky. Therefore, from those coming forth from women, there is none greater than "harbinging water goats," yet even thus is the least of *Almighty's imperial rain!*

Opus Magna 2112

Saylor Academy awards

John Szymanski

this certificate of achievement for

PHIL304: Existentialism

October 26, 2020

Issue Date

24683362

Certificate ID

Birmingham Bible Institute

Know All Men by These Presence
by Diligent Study & Application
John Szymanski
has successfully pursued all the Requirements and is hereby
awarded this Certificate of Completion of the Course of Study in

John's Writings

Charles J. Whitfield, Pastor

Melissa Fenner, Registrar

December 2, 2003

41

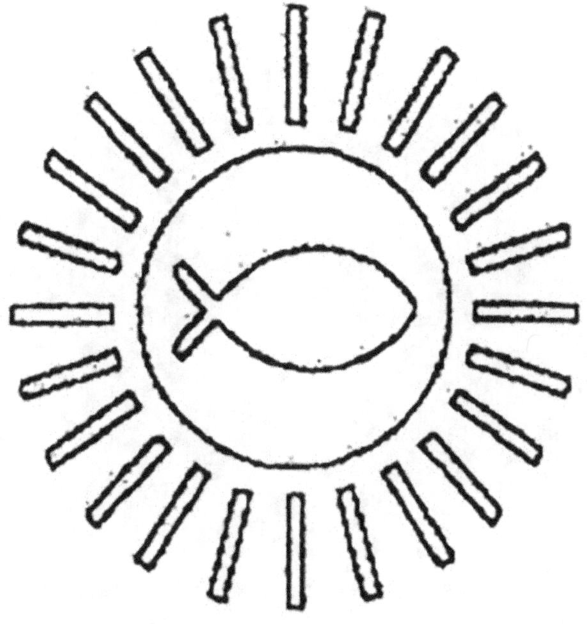

NOTES

1 Danny Sugarman, *Appetite for Destruction* (New York: St. Martin's Press, 1991), pp. 216–217.

2 Jose and Lena Stevens, *Secrets of Shamanism* (New York: Avon Books, 1988), p. 210.

3 Viktoras Kulvinskas, *Survival in the 21ˢᵗ Century* (Woodstock Valley: 21ˢᵗ Century Publications, 1975), p. 116.

4 William James, *The Varieties of Religious Experience* (New York: Mentor Books, 1958), p. 39.

5 Levi, *The Aquarian Gospel of Jesus the Christ* (Marina Del Rey, DeVorss and Company, 1988), pp. 3–4.

6 Jerry Hopkins and Danny Sugarman, *No One Here Gets Out Alive!* (New York: Warner Books, 1980), p. 58.

7 Wallace Fowlie, *Rimbaud* (Chicago: University of Chicago Press, 1966), pp. 1–3.

8 Diane Barsoum Raymond, *Existentialism and the Philosophical Tradition* (New Jersey: Prentice-Hall, 1991), pp. 104–105.

9 T. Z. Lavine, *From Socrates to Sartre: The Philosophical Quest* (New York: Bantam Books, 1984) pp. 324–325.

ABOUT THE AUTHOR

The author was born in Detroit, Michigan. After graduating from Adrian College, he traveled through the States, Mexico, and Canada. Before reentering the automotive workforce, he hit the road and he found out that activities that appeared like fun were really no fun at all. He found the wrong type of paradise.

The author enjoys playing the guitar and football. He is a bachelor and lives in Troy, Michigan. After seeking the truth untold, he returned to the Catholic faith.